# Foreword

The photographic life of this book spans eight days in February, 1968. Marines of the 26th Regiment entrenched at Khe Sanh were under constant harassing fire from two North Vietnamese Army divisions concealed in the surrounding mountains. One adapted quickly to showers of rockets and mortar bombs exploding within the narrow perimeter. It became a life made richer by common sharing of everyday events: dividing equally the can of fruit cocktail in a C-ration; tasting a few minutes more of life, helmet-to-helmet in a slit trench with a man who was a stranger before the barrage began—then suddenly he was closer to you than your brother; watching Death roam again among you, and accepting His choice without too deep astonishment that you were once more spared.

All of these pictures were taken within the Khe Sanh Combat Zone, which includes a nearby fortified hilltop—861 Alpha—part of the screening defenses of Khe Sanh itself, with its metal-slabbed airfield. Helicopters shuttle between the two outposts, when fog and in-coming fire are not too dense. The day after my arrival at Khe Sanh, the enemy launched a pre-dawn probing attack against 861 Alpha—leaving more than twenty Marines crumpled dead and wounded in their trenches and more than fifty North Vietnamese soldiers scattered dead in the barbed wire around the Marines' foxholes.

In these pages, if a man lies uncovered upon the ground he is a North Vietnamese soldier, just fallen, soon to be buried by the Marines. If a man on the ground or a litter has been covered with a poncho, he is a Marine killed in action, awaiting evacuation to the rear and the journey to his family. Not much more can be done, in war, for the dead of either side.

The battlefield is a world of final simplicity.

# I PROTEST!

BY **DAVID DOUGLAS DUNCAN**

A Signet Broadside Published by The New American Library

Photographs and Text:
DAVID DOUGLAS DUNCAN

Design:
WILLIAM GREGORY
PAUL BACON
DAVID DOUGLAS DUNCAN

Copy-editing:
IRENE KASK
RUTH RANDALL


The quotation preceding the photographs is taken from *A Passionate Prodigality* by Guy Chapman. Copyright 1933, © 1965, 1966 by Guy Chapman. Reprinted by permission of Holt, Rinehart and Winston, Inc.

Signet trademark reg. U.S. Pat. Off. and foreign countries
Registered trademark—marca registrada
Hecho en Chicago, U.S.A.

SIGNET BOOKS
are published by The New American Library, Inc.,
1301 Avenue of the Americas, New York, New York 10019

FIRST PRINTING, APRIL, 1968

PRINTED IN THE UNITED STATES OF AMERICA

## by David Douglas Duncan

# I Protest!

For more than the last quarter century I've been shot at by any number of extremely unattractive men, the bulk of them Communists. I'm no peace-nik, Vietnik, pinkie, Commie, liberal, conservative, kook, hippie, hawk or dove. I'm just a veteran combat photographer and foreign correspondent who cares intensely about my country and the role we are playing—and as-signing to ourselves—in the world of today. And I want to shout a loud and clear protest at what has happened at Khe Sanh, and in all of Vietnam.

I have just returned from Khe Sanh, where the 26th Marine Regiment is dug in and holding a narrow valley perimeter set between towering jungle-matted mountain ridges in which an estimated twenty to thirty thousand North Vietnamese soldiers are easing ever forward toward the Marines' barbed wire, apparently waiting for a propitious moment to launch an all-out human-wave attack. General Giap has promised to deliver Khe Sanh as a trophy of war to Hanoi. In Washington, President Lyndon Johnson called together his Joint Chiefs of Staff and demanded that they sign an affidavit stating their convictions that Khe Sanh would never fall to Giap—which absolves the civilian brass if the military are proved wrong.

The Marines behind the sandbags at Khe Sanh were not overjoyed to be designated defenders of the national faith by the President's manifesto-sign-ing political device. They view it as a pistol at their heads and a challenge to Giap to turn Khe Sanh into another Dienbienphu. They call Khe Sanh "The Duck Farm"—with themselves sitting targets for Giap's gunners. Until recently they were ordered by Saigon not to patrol beyond their golf-links-size perimeter—a strategy of General William Westmoreland (former chief of the U.S. Military Advisory Command for Vietnam, now reassigned to Washington) aimed at inducing the Communists to attack and be annihi-lated under a holocaust of artillery shells, aerial bombs and the total fire-power of the encircled Marines themselves. The Marines' thanks and bless-ings go out to the transport crewmen who supply them and to the airmen and artillerymen who maintain constant pressure on the enemy through pro-tective air strikes and shelling. Only America can afford this bankruptcy of tactics—defense through deluge. According to the Pentagon, more explo-sives have been dropped around tiny Khe Sanh than on any other target in the entire history of aerial warfare, including the atomic bomb that incin-erated Hiroshima.

But even if Giap never launches that final attack to breach the wire at the heart of the perimeter, he will have won at Khe Sanh, in the fullest military sense, by having drawn a reinforced Marine regiment—together with tremendous air and artillery fire—away from Westmoreland at a time of desperate troop shortages throughout Vietnam, and then having encircled and immobilized it in the most remote corner of the country beyond all reasonable support and supply—to the Marines' frustrated fury.

The 26th Marines, with whom I spent more than a week of long nights and days, are assigned to combat duty in a place not of their choosing, a place where they are not permitted to fight according to their training and abilities—but which place they will defend with their total professional strength for so long as they are there, and alive. Curiously, being trapped inside their barbed-wire perimeter, surrounded by an enemy free to move at will through the surrounding jungle, made me think of the island campaigns during World War II, when the Japanese were based on Pacific atolls awaiting the Marines' amphibious assaults from the surrounding sea —upon which they were free to maneuver in all directions. Today, the Marines are being forced into defensive battle measures while the North Vietnamese and Viet Cong are employing tactics perfected by Marines. Yet not one Marine whom I met at Khe Sanh spoke of abandoning that forsaken valley to the enemy, and the jungle rats which infest the bunkers. They just dug always deeper into the red earth, piling more sandbags alongside their trenches, cleaned their weapons and got increasingly filthier as the red dust and swirling mist coated them in grime from which there was no escape. And they waited for Charles (professionally respectful) with every weapon aimed at the nearby jungle-fringed mountain and across the plateau, knowing that only *they* can settle the matter when the final countdown comes after Giap has blown the whistle. And Giap has time.

The Marines in their mist-enshrouded trenches at Khe Sanh are living on a time bomb. General Giap now has an army far removed from those early days when his men depended on such primitive devices as excrement-coated bamboo spikes buried in well-used trails to slow our American advance across the land. His men, today, are well equipped. They are undeniably taking a tremendous beating—by our standards of losses—from air and artillery strikes supporting Khe Sanh. But so did the Chinese, at the Yalu River in 1950. Yet they bowed their heads and *walked* straight through our most concentrated fire, to throw us out of North Korea.

According to President Johnson, Secretary of State Rusk, former Secretary of Defense McNamara and General Westmoreland, the purpose of establishing the strongpoint at Khe Sanh was to implant a blocking force at the confluence of supply roads and trails leading into South Vietnam from the Ho Chi Minh Trail in neighboring Laos. The old French Route Colonial Number Nine was the main artery of this logistical network, and (on paper and operations maps in Saigon and Washington) it could be interdicted by basing the Marine garrison at Khe Sanh. In reality, as soon as the Marines appeared at Khe Sanh (over a year ago), the enemy began developing secondary trails as supply routes, anticipating the day when Route Nine would be denied them. The enemy never appeared at Khe Sanh in those days, and our Marines were beguiled into a false sense of security in their seemingly enemy-ignored Shangri-la. They lived aboveground in tents, mess halls and officers clubs. Apparently no one thought of wasting time by digging trenches, filling sandbags or going down out of sight into bunkers—not even for the airstrip control center or the battalion aid stations.

General Westmoreland ordered the Marines to Khe Sanh at a time when construction of McNamara's famed DMZ "Barrier" had the highest priority for all available timber, barbed wire and Seabee construction gangs. Yet only sheer laziness on the part of the Marines deprived them of the protection of deep foxholes—dug by hand in every war. Now it is too late, for those men already dead.

The Marines are trapped in a relatively narrow valley devoid of any natural cover. This exposed place, which the President has chosen as the symbol of our American presence and honor in Vietnam, was the site of a French army fort during colonial days. The Marines occupy the same old French positions—well marked on every North Vietnamese artillery map. The only road leading into Khe Sanh from the supporting military depots at the rear has long been cut. There is one airstrip at Khe Sanh. It is closed each time a plane gets hit (often) and whenever mist, fog or clouds reduce visibility to zero (every night and most days until almost noon). Khe Sanh is six miles from "neutral" Laos, from which sanctuary the enemy pours supplies and replacements into South Vietnam and the siege of Khe Sanh. The jungle cover, three rain-forest tiers deep, conceals most of Giap's activities from aerial surveillance, and the forest foliage also renders some of our artillery shelling and aerial bombing ineffective: bombs and shells detonate among upper branches. Besides, the North Vietnamese and Viet Cong are masters at camouflage and movement along the forest trails. They are not, however, particularly effective guerrillas, being hopelessly book-bound, unable to adapt themselves to fluid combat. They assassinate and mutilate with precision, but they react conventionally when attacked or when their timetables go awry. Indeed, rather than guerrillas, they are just regular military units who campaign by night—using the cover of darkness as a weapon. Fijians or Gurkhas would cut them to ribbons in their own jungles in no time at all. Yet, for all of their shortcomings as guerrillas, the North Vietnamese and Viet Cong do rather well against us—if only because we are conducting such an inept jungle war, on their terms, while seemingly determined to shun all the bitter lessons learned by the French—which they also ignored until it was too late.

The significance of our frustrations at Khe Sanh goes beyond discredited military strategy. It goes beyond the fact that the three senior government civilians who originated America's *war* policy for Vietnam—President Johnson, Secretary of State Rusk and former Secretary of Defense McNamara—lack any kind of field combat experience and so, to them, warfare is a matter of top-secret papers and maps and briefings—and no reality. Judging by evidence from around the rest of the world—the non-Communist world—one conclusion is now inescapable regarding this war. Despite all of the Hanoi oil depots in flames, all of the dropped bridges, every MiG-21 shot down, all of our lost fighter-bomber pilots and those boots of dead paratroopers, and even my heroic, trapped friends at Khe Sanh—despite all of this, there is one fact that must be faced. By standing up to us Americans, with our incredible military power, industrial wealth and men under arms, and with reserves of more of everything still uncommitted to battle ... by just standing up to us and absorbing each body punch we throw, the Viet Cong and the North Vietnamese have beaten us in the eyes of the rest of the world—even if every one of their soldiers should die in his sandals, tonight. We may destroy them and their slender jungle land beyond recall of the slightest glimmer of life for a hundred years—and they still will be the victors. Because they stood—forget their credo—against the most powerful nation ever to exist on the face of the earth, and, in the end, it was they, the simple rice farmers and fishermen and their children, who were stronger.

We Americans may still be reluctant to admit our defeat at the hands of such an "enemy" for fear of losing "face." Face! For nearly three years we have been conducting all-out war. Anyone who thinks that the employment of the entire military establishment of the U.S.—involving atomic aircraft carriers, hydrogen bombers and everything except the ultimate weapon Itself—isn't all-out war is a sadly informed citizen. Two hundred million Americans trying to crush a peasant nation of eighteen million halfway around the earth retain very little "face" in the esteem of this world in which we live. The war is devouring the long roots of our relationships with those nations who have been our firm allies and friends. It is under-mining our economic stability, tarnishing our national character—and sac-rificing our youth. And that is why I left the Marines at Khe Sanh, to protest. Today, defiant and surly—and self-righteous—America stands nearly alone. Johnson and Rusk stubbornly ignore many of us and much of the rest of this deeply concerned world. They conduct their anti-Communist crusade in our name—with our lives, treasure and honor. *I protest!* I have been exposed to probably more Communist gunfire than ever was aimed at the entire Cabinet, Joint Chiefs of Staff and Westmoreland combined, and the Com-munists don't frighten me in the slightest. Their political world was unrav-eling—from defecting Rumania, to Red Guard-torn China, to Communist purging Indonesia—while we escalated toward a military fiasco in Vietnam.

Tragically, it appears that in this election year the war has also become a weapon being used in domestic politics. Thus, one must look long and hard not only at Lyndon Johnson, Rusk and Westmoreland but also at the Congress of the United States, which, with just two dissenting votes, gave the President the authority to take "all necessary steps, including the use of armed force," to defend our commitment in Southeast Asia. This support came in response to what were presented as unprovoked attacks on two of our destroyers in the Tonkin Gulf, August 4, 1964—although no ship was actually hit. They were reportedly *threatened* by North Vietnamese PT boats, the contact and identification being made by radar and radio. But that was enough.

Thinking back a few years, I recall no great clamor on Capitol Hill, in the late forties and early fifties, for America to attack the Soviet Union after Red Army fighter pilots bored straight in to *shoot down* our own Air Force reconnaissance bombers flying over international waters of the Arctic Circle off Alaska and Murmansk. Others, patrolling the frontiers of Turkey and even West Germany, were as quickly dispatched by Soviet interceptors. Congress kept its cool in those perilous earlier years—accepting the loss of our planes and the deaths of our pilots as the unfortunate price of cohabiting this troubled planet with the Russians.

But North Vietnam? Threaten *us!* Declare *war?*... Just hit 'em!

Until recently, South Vietnam was a regular whistlestop on many a Congressman's tour for reelection. Saigon and a few field mess halls were "musts." With the *Tet* offensive, most Congressional combat costumes are now in mothballs. No Congressmen visit Con Thien or Khe Sanh to get the latest word from those dirty, wonderful, shot-at Marines—not even for a group picture.

The concept of hanging American prestige and honor and military valor on the defense of Khe Sanh is sad indeed. Equally tragic was the White House-Saigon method of freeing Hué from the North Vietnamese Army and Viet Cong political cadres who occupied that most ancient Vietnamese cultural shrine during the first days of the *Tet* offensive. Prior to *Tet,* and the disaster it brought upon the entire countryside, Hué was viewed as little more than a tourist attraction for American troops based in Vietnam. The students at its university appeared to sympathize with Ho Chi Minh more than Marshal Ky, but that was true in many towns other than Hué. It was a fine place to take Instamatic color shots for the folks at home, proving that a guy really was serving his country in exotic Asia. Hué was of no recorded military importance. Then the Communists grabbed it and dug in, with their own flag unfurled over the city's historic Citadel. And that spelled the destruction of Hué and the death of untold hundreds of its civilians. We Americans pounded the Citadel and surrounding city almost to dust with air strikes, napalm runs, artillery and naval gunfire and the direct cannon fire of tanks and recoilless rifles—a total effort to root out and kill every enemy soldier. Christ! The mind reels at the carnage, cost—and almost fanatical ruthlessness of it all. Wouldn't a siege-blockade have been a more effective, and less wasteful, military tactic? It has been employed only since before the Crusades—those earlier religious wars to the death.

It seemed that so long as a single Communist survived to shoot back at the attacking Marines and South Vietnamese Rangers, Westmoreland would continue to order counter-battery fire, punching every red button in his Saigon command post. Apparently it was intolerable to contemplate having the Viet Cong flag flutter over Hué during the lengthy weeks of blockade that would surely have ensued until a surrender was forced upon the enemy troops holed up in the once sleepy old city. When Kyoto, the religious heart of Japan, was marked for destruction by our Army Air Force during World War II, it was saved at the last moment by Secretary of War Stimson. He had visited Kyoto's shrines long before the war, and he held a protective hand over the tiny pinhead marking just another target on a war room wall map. Assistant Secretary of War John J. McCloy saved classic Rothenberg, Germany, in like manner. As a child in Philadelphia he had fallen in love with an engraving of the romantic medieval town which his mother had brought home from her first trip to Europe. Poor Hué! It had no friends or protectors in Saigon—or anywhere. Now it is gone; scattered Communists still snipe from the rubble, and our Marine dead are on their way home. Now, too, a fresh North Vietnamese division is reportedly moving toward Hué—seemingly bent upon besieging the Americans setting up housekeeping in the ruins.

Hué, of course, was but one of the many cities being destroyed by the war in

Vietnam. This was once the garden country of Southeast Asia. I vividly recall a cloudless autumn night at Con Thien when I stood near Mike Company's bunker and watched out-going mortars starburst deep in the Demilitarized Zone. A young Marine platoon lieutenant, Joe Williams of Atlanta, Georgia, joined me. We both faced the DMZ in order to spot the pin-flash of fire of the enemy recoilless rifle which had been sporadically blasting our positions—the flash giving us two seconds warning in which to hit the deck. We saw only our own bursting mortars. Joe told me of Khe Sanh (which I'd not yet visited) and of its beauty—high verdant mountain ranges where a Frenchman was experimenting with coffee on a magnificent plantation, of the wildlife (which Joe never shot), especially the great deer and the tigers which roamed the forests, the heavy-bodied, lantern-jawed trout as big as salmon; and of a species of funny little rock monkey which raised hell with the nerves of the Marines by throwing pebbles at them from the forest darkness, scaring the daylights out of everyone.

As Joe spoke of the mysteries and excitement and promises of Khe Sanh, he turned toward me in the gloom. Another star flashed out in the DMZ night behind Joe's back—and with a screeching howl a recoilless shell ripped between us to explode a hundred yards deeper inside the Marines' positions. Joe and I lay laughing on the ground where we had fallen—two slices of hurriedly hacked bread damned near burned in the big toaster. As we lay in the mud trying to dig in deeper without raising our heads, Joe Williams of Atlanta said of Khe Sanh, Vietnam, "If I don't die here, I'd like to come back, someday, to live."

Now, Joe Williams is gone from Vietnam, shot through the leg by a sniper. Now, the gutted cities of this once-pristine country are joined by necklaces of shell holes and bomb craters. Various American agencies in Saigon list the ebb and flood of refugees of every battle, totaling them at the end of the year. There is no column in their charts in which to record the opinions or frame of mind of those refugees whose homes went up in smoke during our self-assigned anti-Communist crusade in their country. Nor is there any list, anywhere, recording the number of civilians killed in Vietnam—South Vietnam—since we arrived to protect them from the horror of life under the invader, Ho Chi Minh. No South Vietnamese villager has ever been known to apply a scorched earth policy by burning his home to prevent its falling into the hands of the Viet Cong—yet the ashes of countless rural and urban houses wash away with each rainstorm that sweeps the land.

I protest the tactics. I protest the destruction. And I protest the war rhetoric of Vietnam. Our spokesmen in Saigon explained the *Tet* offensive this way: By coming out of their holes in everything up to division strength throughout the land to attack various provincial capitals, isolate Saigon, occupy Hué, besiege Khe Sanh and destroy the rural "pacification" program, the Viet Cong and North Vietnamese Army revealed their *weakness;* their all-out assault was nothing but a death gasp born of desperation in the face of our "victories." I, personally, resent being thought so naïve, even downright idiotic. I should have enjoyed having the company of the men who dreamed up this explanation of our shining Vietnam successes of recent weeks while easing my aging bones into various foxholes and trenches around Khe Sanh—with 122-millimeter Chinese-made rockets persuasively growling at my heels. I resent people trying to sell military victories and defeats the same way they pitch 101-millimeter cigarettes, shaving cream and deodorants.

Another prime example of the Pentagon hucksters' handiwork is that smooth and, surprisingly, widely accepted and printed tag, "Free World Forces," used to categorize the "Allied" military units deployed in South Vietnam. What they really mean is that approximately one-half million American military men are in South Vietnam—with General Westmoreland reportedly asking for two hundred thousand more ( A fresh tactic to escalate another division or two, avoiding public outcries?). In addition, there are roughly six hundred thousand South Vietnamese, wholly subsidized—and armed—by Washington. Another forty-eight thousand soldiers have come from rebuilt and U.S.-aid-supported South Korea—not exactly a totally independent "Free World" nation. Add something like fifteen thousand Thais, fully equipped with American weapons and sent by a government receiving a massive military dole from the United States; a couple of thousand Filipinos, grateful for the American military aid which helps keep a lately resurgent Huk rebellion in its place; another eight thousand Australians—free of American domination in every sense, yet deeply aware of the white man's precarious role and future in Asia...as are the final "Free World Forces" from New Zealand, perhaps fifteen hundred men. Those of us who are a bit older, who spent foxhole time in the heartbreak early months of Korea, remember an era when "Allied" meant sharing chow and risks with military units from Great Britain, France, Ethiopia, Colombia, Turkey and a tough fistful of other battle groups from all over the truly free world.

A couple of days after the *Tet* offensive had rolled the "Free World Forces" back on their heels, General Westmoreland appeared before the hundreds of foreign correspondents assembled in Saigon, to brief them and to answer some of their questions regarding the seeming debacle. Handsome, proud and unshaken, eyes flashing under the TV lights, immaculate in short-sleeved, crisply pressed khaki, and articulate in his mastery of details concerning every recent battle and others still in progress, the General was most impressive. Then, for me at least, he ruined it. He spoke of the Viet Cong-North Vietnamese Army attacks in language which made one feel that the General truly viewed himself as the defender of some mystic religious-military order, and that the war he was fighting was being conducted under holy rules of battle and honor which the enemy had now violated by attacking during the *Tet* New Year celebrations. Worse, he sounded and appeared like the senior scoutmaster of all time, standing there before us and almost petulantly complaining that the bad guys had cheated, winning their merit badges by shoddy means. To be specific, General Westmoreland accused the enemy of launching their offensive with "deceit, treachery, and total disregard for innocent civilian lives." Deceit? Treachery? Did not a general named George Washington cross the Delaware River to surprise the enemy on that holiest of Christian nights—Christmas, 1776? And innocent civilian lives? How much regard did we Americans have for them on August 6, 1945, at Hiroshima—a city of approximately half a million inhabitants and no military significance?

At his press conference, General Westmoreland spoke of five thousand eight hundred "confirmed enemy soldiers" being killed during the first few days of the *Tet* city-offensive. He also mentioned twenty-five hundred Vietnamese being captured, adding his opinion that while the majority of the prisoners would prove to be Viet Cong soldiers masquerading as townspeople, a high percentage of the detainees would undoubtedly prove to be innocent civilians, and would be released. This appraisal of Giap's casualties by General Westmoreland left just one nagging question. What percentage of the fifty-eight hundred "confirmed Viet Cong" could logically be assumed to have been innocent civilians caught in the same urban battle zones—before death silenced their ability to vindicate themselves?

In a later interview granted the Associated Press, General Westmoreland summed up the results of the *Tet* offensive. His appraisal of the combat situation seemed unrelated to our military posture at that moment in South Vietnam:

"By committing a large share of his forces to a major offensive, the enemy achieved some tactical surprise. This offensive has required us to react and to modify our plans in order to take advantage of the opportunity to inflict heavy casualties upon him. Although the enemy has achieved some temporary psychological advantage, he suffered a military defeat."

Finally, as the worst example of the Vietnam war rhetoric, there is something so fundamentally offensive to Marines everywhere that it is rarely discussed with outsiders. It was forced upon them by the Department of Defense—and they feel it is degrading and humiliating them as Marines and as human beings. Their shame—and it should be our national shame—rests on the only two words being used to distinguish between victory and defeat in the war in-Vietnam: "Body Count."

Every "Free World Forces" press conference reeks with these two words; each American Armed Forces broadcast is prefaced by the "Body Count" of that day's action; all records of every skirmish or major campaign feature, above everything else, "Body Count." It is inescapable, insidious, corrosive—even among veterans of other wars, where victory was represented by hilltops overrun, sea walls breached then bypassed, islands secured and cities captured and whole armies taken prisoner. Who, in the name of God and decency, can remember anyone posting daily "Body Count" scores during the battles for Salerno, Iwo Jima, Omaha Beach, Remagen Bridge, Stalingrad or even Berlin. But, now! Someone, apparently in Washington, decided that there *must* be a way to keep score in a war where there are no victories, ever, in the conventional meaning of the word as related to combat. If "Body Count" is considered victory, does it mean we threaten genocide to all who oppose us and our arms and our political philosophy?

Admit it—and dislike it—or not, but we Americans appear to be sinking into a quagmire of grim impressions being created about ourselves—by ourselves—which may soon cast us in the character of the bullyboys (the neo-Aryan master race) of the coming generation. We seem determined to impose our will and way of life upon most of the rest of the world, whether or not they want it, appreciate it or ask for it. We justify this dispatch of military and economic missionaries in the name of nation-building, and the protection of our vital spheres of interest across the face of the globe, everywhere—especially if anyone can produce even circumstantial evidence that Communists (of any color or breed) might be interested in the place. I protest selling *fear,* of anybody, as America's foreign policy.

We land troops in Santo Domingo and Saigon; we lose hydrogen bombs off Spain and Greenland; we awaken to discover our snooper ships have been trapped off the Sinai Desert and North Korea; we flood the entire world with monstrous embassy staffs, then threaten to stop American tourists—our best ambassadors of all—from wandering around the world, even though most of the dollars they spend abroad are actually said to return home rather quickly in the form of export purchases. We scoff at the claim of the Russians that they hold free elections, then act offended when others raise eyebrows at the results of our shotgun wedding of military junta and free elections in Saigon—where the opposition candidates were hand-picked and screened by us, and the Viet Cong candidates were out in their jungle foxholes with their rifles, the only ballots still persuasive in that tortured land.

Probably few Americans will see a film made for the Bertrand Russell "American War Crime Trials" propaganda extravaganza in Stockholm last autumn. One would expect to dismiss it as blatant Communist propaganda, too, but it doesn't work quite like that. It runs for seventeen uninterrupted minutes without a soundtrack. The film—black and white—is of rather poor technical quality, which is understandable when one learns it was made from copies of TV films, newsreels, magazine and newspaper photos. There is no footage made by any Communist cameraman, no photo made by a Communist photographer. Every inch of the film was made by Western, non-Communist newsmen working for our television, magazine or news-paper services. And the film is a heartbreaker, so appalling as to defy total mental recall by a professional reporter. It shows American and South Vietnamese soldiers torturing, beating, mutilating Viet Cong and suspected Viet Cong prisoners; others, dead, are dragged off triumphantly behind tanks and amtracs. Villages, of course, are razed and burned; babies are left dying—also burned; and there isn't a sound from the screen. The film-makers obtained no permission from the Western agencies owning the rights to the original shots—in fact the pictures were all pirated. So these seventeen minutes will probably never be seen on any commercial Ameri-can TV or theater screen. But they should. For then each of us would un-derstand what truly hideous acts have taken place in the name of bringing democracy and "our way of life" to South Vietnam.

Many of us in America, at least men of my generation, can still clearly recall those early terrible newsreels made in Greece and Yugoslavia and Germany itself during the Hitler era. Now, one such newsreel exists which shows American atrocities in Vietnam. Every American would be disbe-lieving and aghast at seeing the film for himself. Of course, no one has really known—just as surely as many Germans did not know—but I am tell-ing you all, now, that the film exists, that the pictures were made by non-Communist newsmen, and that ignorance will be no excuse or defense when the film finally surfaces in this country... as it assuredly will. And there will be no refuge in the argument that our random acts of bestiality were pardonable because enemy atrocities were politically motivated, and even more gruesome.

By comparison to what is happening to *us,* the future of the war in Vietnam seems simple, and a solution easy. The President of the United States has asked us all, "What would you do if you were here in my place, as President?" Well, Mr. President, I would do three things without delay:

1) I would immediately order the complete cessation of bombing of North Vietnam, *with whom we are not at war.* We might still regain a fraction of our lost respect in this world community while, I hope, there is something left to salvage.

2) I would order all fighter and bomber crews to concentrate on Viet Cong and North Vietnamese Army installations and routes of supply in *South* Vietnam until a cease-fire is secured. One might imagine the relief of our pilots at being assigned targets reasonably uncluttered by such operational inconveniences as SAMs and antiaircraft fire, and even air-to-air missiles fired by the few surviving MiGs in North Vietnam.

3) I would ask the United Nations to sponsor and police a referendum to be held throughout all of South Vietnam. The referendum would pose only three questions of the South Vietnamese populace:

a) Do you wish to unite into a single state with North Vietnam?

b) Do you wish to remain a separate and independent state?

c) If you wish to remain a separate and independent state, do you wish the assistance of the Americans in your task of nation-building?

Upon these answers, Mr. President, I would base my future policy and conduct of the war in South Vietnam. I would then concentrate on finding an honorable and stable role for the United States of America in the world of tomorrow.

But there is very little time.

**This book is dedicated
to
that silent day
when
the war stops**

*Few had forebodings of their destiny. At the halts they lay in the long wet grass and gossiped, enormously at ease. The whistle blew. They jumped for their equipment. The little grey figure of the colonel far ahead waved its stick. Hump your pack and get a move on. The next hour, man, will bring you three miles closer to your death. Your life and your death are nothing to these fields—nothing, no more than it is to the man planning the next attack at G.H.Q. You are not even a pawn. Your death will not make the world safe for your children. Your death means no more than if you had died in your bed, full of years and respectability, having begotten a tribe of young. Yet by your courage in tribulation, by your cheerfulness before the dirty devices of this world, you have won the love of those who have watched you. All we remember is your living face, and that we loved you for being of our clay and spirit.*

Guy Chapman
*Magnicourt-sur-Canche, France*
*21 October, 1916*

from A PASSIONATE PRODIGALITY

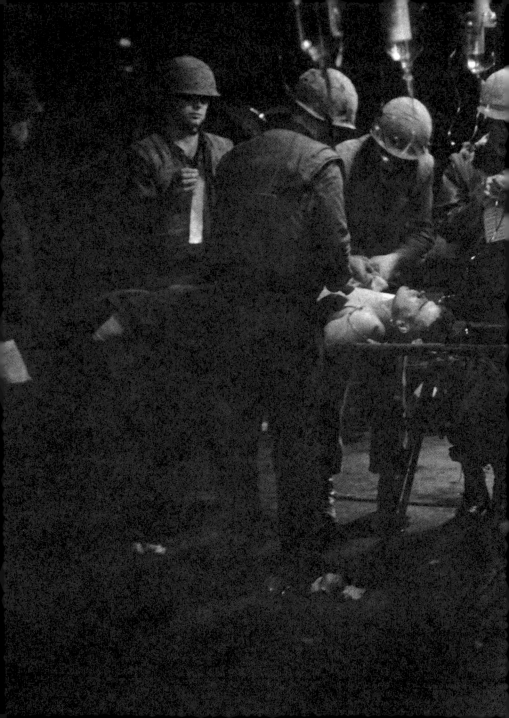

*All we remember is your living face,
and that we loved you for being of our clay and spirit*

# Acknowledgments and Photographic data

All of the photographs made in Vietnam during my most recent assignment to that shattered country were taken for *Life* Magazine and ABC-TV News. Elmer Lower, President of ABC-News, and George Hunt, Managing Editor of *Life*—old friends—are sponsoring my current work in Southeast Asia, and I thank them both. I also want to express my deepest appreciation and thanks to Stephen Gelman, who suggested cuts in my original manuscript (written in thirty-six nonstop hours the week after I returned from Khe Sanh), bringing it down to a more manageable length, and deleting some expressions that were perhaps too harsh in their bitterness. The opinions and conclusions in this book are, of course, mine alone.

Very little has changed in combat photography—at least for me—between the battlefields of Vietnam, today, and the front lines of Korea, in 1950. The weather in Vietnam seems easier to bear—although some troopers claim they would rather face the paralyzing horror of another Chosin Reservoir winter than confront the leeches and malaria and man-swallowing muck of the rice paddies and jungles, day after day, during their year's combat tour in Vietnam.

Once again, I depend upon two Leicas (custom-built M3Ds), crossed bandolier-style on my chest. One Leica is fitted with a Leitz 50mm FI.4 Summilux lens, and the other with a Canon 25mm F3.5 lens. Both lenses are fitted with medium yellow filters. In addition—hanging down the center of my chest—I carry a Nikon-F with a Nikor 200mm F4 lens, also fitted with a medium yellow filter. The film is Kodak Tri-X, developed in Kodak D-76 at the *Life* Magazine photo-lab in New York. All processing is under the direction of *Life*'s chief of photographic laboratories, George Karas, and *Life*'s chief laboratory technician, Mauro Rubino. The matched enlargements (11″ x 14″) were made by Carmine Ercolano, Stephen Esoff and Marten Olsen. These master craftsmen at *Life* printed the final, balanced set of photographs for this book during off-hours—which meant staying in the darkroom until nearly dawn several mornings. They helped me out of friendship, and no other reason.

Except for cameras, helmet and flak jacket, my only equipment is a webbed pistol belt on which I hang two canteens (one on each hip), a sheath knife and four ammo-clip pouches (two on either side of the belt buckle, each holding five 35mm film cans apiece). Cleated dead center into the back of the webbed belt—touching my tail bone—there is a medical corpsman's three-pouched, waterproof, unfolding supply kit. In one pouch I store approximately fifty rolls of 35mm Tri-X, specially sealed in discarded Ektachrome cans by my darkroom friends at *Life*. If I sink into a rice paddy, or flood out in the monsoon rains, my film remains safe and dry. In the other two pouches I carry an extra pair of socks, an extra pair of skivvy shorts, a towel, razor, bar of soap, toothbrush and toothpaste, an extra pocket-size notebook, a pair of binoculars and a sub-miniature radio —all in plastic, waterproof bags. (Other than lead, naturally, water constitutes the greatest hazard to photographic work in Vietnam.) As for my gear, that's it, except for a fabulous, aluminum unipod camera-clamp (custom-built by my old World War II Marine friend, Var Keljik, of St. Paul, Minnesota), a waterproof flashlight and a deep-sea diver's luminous-dial wrist compass, which is never removed. Someday I may want to know directions in a hurry—without stopping to inquire the way of local characters, familiar with every nearby jungle path.

D.D.D.
Sunday
St. Patrick's Day
17 March, 1968
New York City

# About the author

Born in Kansas City, Missouri, an archaeology major (University of Arizona) and a graduate of the University of Miami (B.A. in zoology and Spanish), David Douglas Duncan has since 1938 roamed the world as a photographer, foreign correspondent, combat cameraman and art historian. He holds the rank of lieutenant colonel (retired) in the United States Marine Corps, where he was decorated with the Legion of Merit, Distinguished Flying Cross, Air Medal with three clusters and the Purple Heart.

During World War II, he photographed Marine Corps aviation operations throughout the Pacific, fought with the famed Fijian guerrillas behind enemy lines on Bougainville, filmed Marine fighter-bomber attacks against Japanese pillboxes on Okinawa (shooting his pictures from inside a plexiglass-nosed capsule slung beneath the wing of a single-seat P-38 fighter plane). Duncan made the first landing upon the Japanese mainland, photographed the surrender ceremonies aboard the U.S.S. *Missouri* in Tokyo Bay and accompanied the initial Marine occupation force to enter Peking in the autumn of 1945—just as Nationalist China erupted in civil war.

In 1946, as a *Life* Magazine photographer, Duncan took his cameras to Palestine, reporting from the center of terrorist battles between Jews and the British Army. In 1947, he was the only Western photographer to cover the Red Army take-over of Bulgaria. That summer, he stood in the middle of communal riots in India, where Hindus and Moslems were butchering each other. 1949 found Dave Duncan in war-torn Greece, recording the atrocities left in the wake of Communist efforts to conquer the Hellenic peninsula.

When the Korean War exploded in June, 1950, Duncan was there, documenting the ordeal of the Marines on the Naktong River summer perimeter and their December withdrawal from the freezing Chosin Reservoir. Duncan was the last man to be evacuated from Hungnam when the United Nations armies were forced to abandon North Korea. His book on Marines in combat, *This Is War!*, has been called by Edward Steichen "the greatest photographic document ever produced showing men in war." During the spring and summer of 1951, Duncan traced the decline of the British Empire in Asia—from Hong Kong to Burma, Malaya, India and Iran. In May, 1952, he took the first pictures—from the Baltic to Bavaria—showing the birth of the Iron Curtain in Europe (in 1947 he had made similar photographs disclosing the barbed wire and machine-gun barricades raised by the Russians between Soviet Armenia and eastern Turkey).

When Major General Mohammed Naguib and a young colonel, Gamal Abdel Nasser, forced King Farouk to abdicate the throne of Egypt, in July, 1952, David Duncan photographed and wrote the story from inside coup headquarters in Cairo. For the next six months of 1952, he tracked Communist agents through western Europe, East Berlin and East Vienna, proving they were purchasing embargoed strategic Western war material and shipping it to the Soviet Union. Throughout the spring and summer of 1953 he aimed his cameras and typewriter at the French colonial war in Southeast Asia and predicted "Indochina All But Lost"—nine months before the fall of Dienbienphu. In 1956, having left *Life*, Duncan joined a multi-nationality volunteer force helping the Hungarian refugees fleeing Budapest. He worked with the Knights of Malta (without taking a picture) that Christmas and New Year on the Austro-Hungarian frontier, his last contact with warfare until returning to Vietnam in the summer of 1967. The eleven years between wars were filled with photographing art subjects and writing *The Private World of Pablo Picasso, The Kremlin and Its Treasures,* and *Picasso's Picassos.* Shortly before his latest trip to Vietnam—after five years of work—he published his word-and-picture autobiography, *Yankee Nomad.*